T0369939

Four Days in Algeria

FOUR DAYS IN ALGERIA

poems

∾

Clarence Major

Red Hen Press | *Pasadena, CA*

Book design by Mark E. Cull.

Library of Congress Cataloging-in-Publication Data

Names: Major, Clarence, author.
Title: Four days in Algeria: poems / Clarence Major.
Description: First edition. | Pasadena, CA: Red Hen Press, 2025.
Identifiers: LCCN 2024018861 | ISBN 9781636281780 (trade paperback) | ISBN
    9781636282473 (hardcover) | ISBN 9781636281797 (ebook)
Subjects: LCGFT: Poetry.
Classification: LCC PS3563.A39 F68 2025 | DDC 811/.54—dc23/eng/20240429
LC record available at https://lccn.loc.gov/2024018861

Acknowledgments:
"The End of the World" appeared in *The New Yorker*, November 15, 2021.

The National Endowment for the Arts, the Los Angeles County Arts Commission,
the Ahmanson Foundation, the Dwight Stuart Youth Fund, the Max Factor Family
Foundation, the Pasadena Tournament of Roses Foundation, the Pasadena Arts &
Culture Commission and the City of Pasadena Cultural Affairs Division, the City
of Los Angeles Department of Cultural Affairs, the Audrey & Sydney Irmas Chari-
table Foundation, the Meta & George Rosenberg Foundation, the Albert and Elaine
Borchard Foundation, the Adams Family Foundation, Amazon Literary Partner-
ship, the Sam Francis Foundation, and the Mara W. Breech Foundation partially
support Red Hen Press.

First Edition
Published by Red Hen Press
www.redhen.org

I am not less poet; I am more conscious of all that
I am, am not, and might become.
—Jean Toomer

CONTENTS

Four Days in Algeria

TOURISTS

I lean over and whisper love in your ear.
Your hands are folded on the table,
but you are not praying.
All the shops are closed.

It is siesta time.
You put down your wine glass
and spread a tourist map out on the table.
With your index finger
you point to a place on the map.
It is where we are.
 I suddenly see us on the map—
tiny figures, sitting in front of a café—this one.

We finish the wine.
The one that is me calls the tiny waiter,
pays him,
and we stand, walk away, a bit woozy,

down the map-street, holding hands—
two happy people in love,
with a whole city left to explore,
and we have a good map to guide us.

August in Paris

I'm on the balcony. It's three o'clock.
Below, I see a line of cars in purple shadows
of tall stately buildings on this quiet afternoon,
 cars parked bumper-to-bumper,
some with wheels up on the narrow sidewalk.
They are like ancient relics
left by an extinct tribe thousands of years ago.
A single formation of blue-gray clouds
floating high above, indifferently, against a yellowish sky.
Across the street, all the jealousies are shut
as if everyone is away permanently on holiday.
It's as though if I go out into the city
I'd have the avenues and boulevards to myself—
but what good is that?
 Museums and restaurants closed till five.
At five, I venture out—for yet another exploration.

I'VE JUST CHECKED IN

This is a view from the hotel window
of the afternoon rush hour with cars bumper-to-bumper
 and harsh sunlight throwing long shadows ahead of them.
I look directly down at the tops of people
walking along the sidewalk. I see heads on shoulders,
 legs moving forward and back, like scissors,
a bird's-eye-view of human bodies in motion,
 their shadows preceding them along the sidewalk.
Just now one dashes across the street to the other side,
dodging busy traffic, causing a taxi driver to blast his horn
 repeatedly, showing his disapproval.
Would I rather be in a quieter place, a place with rolling hills of grass
and endless skies blue as robin's eggs?
No, not at this moment.
This is the intensity, the throbbing sense of life,
that I have bargained for.

10:30 P.M.

Night and the intersection below
with lighted cars zooming by,
whirring sirens occasionally—this is Paris.
Jealousies across the boulevard
all closed except one—open to a dimly lighted room.
On my tiny balcony I lean on the wrought iron railing
looking down at the busyness. Behind me,
inside my room, folded *Herald* on armchair,
a cup of warm tea on bedside table.
Madam Patrice sweetly left a vase of tulips
on the stand in the corner. Strangely,
I don't miss the night silence of my hometown.
 It's odd, but sirens all night, especially on weekends,
are somehow reassuring—of what, I don't know—
perhaps that everybody is awake and alert.

One O'Clock in Florence

It's one o'clock and all the shops here
in Florence are closed till three thirty.
We're in the room relaxing till four.
My wife is taking a nap.
She's breathing quietly and evenly.
She's using her left arm as a pillow.
Now she wakes and she tells me her dream.
She's back in college and she nervously enters a school building
where she must take a final exam,
but the minute she enters, it becomes a store here in Florence.
Unamazed, she does some quick shopping—
buys a pretty dress, a pair of sensible shoes, a unique purse,
but when she's ready to leave, she can't find her way out.
Finally, she finds an exit—waking *is* the exit.

Closed on Sunday

They have come out of the ruins
and out of the cathedrals and out of the museums
and are sitting in metal chairs at outdoor coffee shops
and some have not even walked as far as the shops
but have sat down in their shiny gabardine clothes
alongside their fake-leather handbags
and expensive cameras on the stone of the hot balustrade
and the stone steps of government buildings. *Closed on Sunday.*
Some have their sunburned noses stuck in guidebooks,
others, through sunglasses, are scanning brochures.
One is reading the only English language newspaper
he could find in this blisteringly hot country,
so full of other exhausted tourists
where natives speak a language foreign to their ears.

UNDER THE STARS

A night of slow dancing under the stars
and she says I hope this night never ends.
We are belly to belly and I'm worried
she's going to have another accident by stepping
on her long midnight-blue-dress and stumbling,
maybe even falling, but I'm here to catch her,
I'm ready to catch her if she stumbles, if she falls,
and the women at that table in the corner are still watching us,
or maybe watching her only, watching
with admiration or envy or contempt,
as they sip their martinis or something stronger,
gin maybe and grin with glassy eyes. Now the slow music
abruptly stops and the tempo changes to a quick beat.
We stop the belly to belly, stand apart.
The musicians on the stand, happier in the upbeat,
grinning as they gig with delight and
the night is younger than it's ever been.

The Hotel Room

Stark, small, but adequate.
I've just arrived. The city map I bought at the vendor
is spread out on the bed. The telephone
on the bedside table is ringing. I know who is calling.
I will not answer. Gift-wrapped packages are on the table
 alongside the laptop, and the bowl of grapes.
The drapes are pulled back—daylight coming in.
My luggage is on the stand.
I've just turned on the television.
The news is in a language I speak little
Yet I'm here to make the most of my stay.

FISH SOUP

Ancient windows small with crossbars to keep in the warmth.
Moss grows up the sides to the thatched tops.
Little chimneys poke up like Popeye's pipe.
A bird feeder here and there.
Flowers in pots suspended on hooks at front doors.
I pass an open window. A woman in her eighties inside
in thick wool skirts moving about slowly, lighting candles,
setting the table for supper. I smell fish soup cooking.
I stop in the cobbled village square. It's late afternoon.
No one is about. Here is a long-dry fountain
set on a square stone platform. I sit down on its ledge to rest.

Cypresses

In Maria's village the tallest cypresses grow by the cemetery
and alongside the train tracks surrounded by sunflowers
where telephone poles are bent sideways by storms and wind.
Maria says when you buy a house in America
you should plant cypresses, like these here in my village.
 They will remind you of your happy times here in Italy.
I did and they are majestic—the tallest things for miles around.

CADMIUM YELLOW LIGHT

The place is peaceful,
the late morning light shines brightly through upper windows
down across the worn planks of the dirty littered floor.
The serious early morning coffee drinkers have gone.
I sit here with my coffee, making this poem about the shop as it is now.
Paper cups left on tables rather than dropped in trashcans
on the way out. They remain like things
that have never given pleasure to anyone. The girl in the corner
with her computer is writing one final letter to the boyfriend
she feels she must finally ditch. I have three cookies on a plate.
I take a bite out of each. Delicious!
I look at my watch. Suddenly, it's time to go teach.

Beach

The sand is oatmeal-yellow wet
with pockets of blue.
After rain, the sun has come out.
The ocean is restless still.
The sky, packed with rainclouds.
A woman in a colorful kimono walking by
holding a parasol overhead.
Two boys building a castle.
Down on hands and knees,
one looks inside to see
if the duke and the duchess are home.
He sees the servants
up and down a winding staircase,
and down in the kitchen
cooks are preparing supper,
while a woman with a parasol is
knocking at the front door.

A Girl on the Beach

Barefoot, in a white cotton dress,
whipped by the wind, she uses a stick
to draw a self-portrait in the sand.
She bends down, the curve of her back
forms one side of a pyramid,
the other side finishing in sand,
herself a stick-figure with stick arms
accommodating the path of the eye
around and around.
In an hour, rainwater, or the tide,
like a day ago, will wash her away.

Five People

Francis and I watch from afar.
At the gathering of the beggars
on the outskirts of town, under a tree,
they count money snatched or given
and things grabbed or shoplifted.
The booty is piled in a barrel for all to share.
The girl crestfallen watches over a woman likely her mother.
She's stretched out on the ground
with a blanket over her—obviously sick.
Her belly is swollen. Perhaps Crohn's disease or colitis?
Maybe she's pregnant again and about to abort.
Francis says, "In Paris and in Rome they
follow you in the streets and try to snatch your purse or bag.
If they are unsuccessful, they spit on you."
Yes, but the rest of humanity has cast them out,
and they struggle in the trenches,
desperately trying to stay alive.

ARRIVING

We walk out into the bright sunlight and
go toward the noise of the carnival.
A woman in a long pink dress,
with a green shawl thrown across her shoulders,
greets us at the entryway. A little black dog stands at her side
looking up at us, his tongue wagging.
We pay and she stamps the backs of our hands.

SKULLS

I touched Byron's name carved in 1810
into one of the columns of the Temple of Poseidon—
his youthful bid for posterity—he was twenty-two.
He died at age thirty-six.

While on a boat going from one island to another,
a hundred and seventy-four years after Byron's visit to the temple,
I noticed a Greek man staring at me.
He finally said, *you are an American, right?*

I said yes. He said *I lived in America*
for a few years. That is how I knew
you were an American. In America I worked in a restaurant,
but it was difficult to manage, so I returned to my country—

I wanted to be sure to die here, not in America.
And a beautiful country it is, I said.
Be sure to see the monasteries, he said.
I went to the cluster of monasteries in Kalabaka in the deltaic plains.

I looked up. They were perched high on rocks,
 four hundred meters. Before being elevated up,
I watched a monk pulling up buckets of water
 by rope and pully. I too was lifted and was left on my own
to look around. The monastery was an
impressive little village.

I peeked into a dungeon and saw neat rows of
skulls of dead monks on long narrow shelves,
 lined up like books in a library—each highly individual.
 One morning, a day or two later, I sat outside a small café

sipping coffee and eating bread, fruit, and yogurt,
watching an old prostitute marching back and forth
from one end of the block to the other
as men were going to work—none stopped to talk to her.

This had perhaps been her beat for years, but lately
business was not so good. Watching her,
I remembered Byron's graffiti, his early death,
and the skulls—that said *I once existed.*

This Morning

The ocean this morning is ferocious,
but its colors are playful and sparkling—
all washed with a sudsy whiteness splashing foam roughly
all the way up across the yellow sandy beach.
At times like this, I know to keep my distance.
I sit here on this distant rock high above the action,
in awe of the ocean's fury, power, and beauty.

THE END OF THE WORLD

I look out the window
at a silent dark night—a night of blue
and rust with specks of yellow.
Neighborly windows mostly dark.
Entryway across the street, bright.
The front door locked.
Always locked at eleven.
Below my window, under streetlights,
brightly lighted from inside,
a three-car commuter train
quietly slides by, as if on water—
I turn back to the TV.
I'm watching a movie
about the end of the world—
always about to happen.

WINTER MORNING ON THE TERRACE

See, I'm in my heavy wool coat,
my floppy felt hat pulled down over
my ears to keep warm. My fingers
stiff from the chill. The breeze from
the sea coming in briskly, the horizon
impossible to see, water and sky one,
like skin to bone, one nature. The tall
palm trees along the avenue shaken
furiously like prey in the mouth of a predator.
Traffic below, sparse, and slow.

The Lady, the Maid, and the Dog

In 17th century England class was nailed down
firmly like shiplap to drywall.
My persona was a dog-trainer
and the Lady had requested my persona's services.
When my persona arrived,
the Lady was being tended to by her attendant—
her "maid"—a person from the lower classes.
As my persona entered the room
The Lady was holding her nose high
as if sniffing something on the air.
While the lady looked critically at her own face reflected
in a tiny handheld mirror,
her maid arranged her shawl—just so!—
around her shoulders.
The Lady's small dog jumped around impatiently
on the floor beside the hem of her long dress.
He bit the dress and yanked at it.
(Had the butler escorted my persona in too soon—
as these last-minute preparations were taking place?)
The frisky dog—not a bit class-conscious—
stopped chewing on the dress
and dashed quickly over to my persona.
He wagged and my persona patted him on the head.
Ah, my persona thought, this sweet pup will be easy
to train to sit, to fetch, to be a loving lap dog.

HOUSEBOAT

On the river the blue houseboat was a comfort,
a way to get away from the house and routine,
away from the city and city noise and to listen instead
to the river lapping and shifting and to birds cheeping
and see frogs leaping, to sit back on the daybed and read a book
or work on a poem, to stay most of the day.
Occasionally a blackbird on the roof, tapping.
When in those moments I stopped reading or stopped writing
I could look up and see through the little twin windows
on the other side of the river the unraveling road
leading up quickly into an explosion of trees and houses,
all blue and blending with the sky.

CHARACTER

In Venice at the beginning of Carnival
our friends said only tourists take part in Carnival,
but we wanted to experience Carnival—so, we went
to the mask-maker, a little ancient man with a bald head.
His smock was dirty blue, and his eyeglasses were thick.
He sucked on an unlighted pipe sticking out of the side of his mouth.
His shop was no bigger than your average closet.
The walls were crammed full of masks—horrible faces
with disfigured features, goofy and goony faces, thuggish and brutal faces,
dogs-faces, rats-faces, clown faces, pigfaces, frog-faces, faces you don't want to see
on a dark street at night. He was applying paint to a face
he called the face without character. I asked how was that possible.
He said when you wear it, you give it character. I tried it on and looked
in his tiny wall mirror. I became somebody I didn't recognize.

Four Days in Algeria

Three young men from the university
picked me up at the airport and dropped me off
at my hotel in Algiers.
After the long flight from Italy,
I wanted to take a shower, but only two drops of water—
stingily—came out of the shower head.
The Frenchman next door said you must tip the concierge
and he will turn on the water—but you must be quick
because he will turn it off after one hour.

The next day the morning call to prayer woke me.
Very few people were about. The few I saw were solemn.
A man was searching a garbage can.
After I finished my duties at the university,
the Frenchman and I walked to the old city
and down through the narrow winding streets of the Kasbah.
We were the only ones there.

The next day at the entrance of the grand 17th century mosque
he and I took off our shoes respectfully and entered,
as hundreds of men on knees with foreheads to floor
in prayer as we walked through, quietly, and respectfully,
exiting at the other end. Outside, we felt a cool breeze
from the Mediterranean. I thought Fauvist paintings
of the Algerian coast—with their brilliant blues.
Walking around the city, I saw only one woman
whose face was not covered.

One night I went with the Frenchman
to the dining hall of the French Embassy.
The Algerian bartender pleasantly served
the European men whisky, beer, and wine.
When I stood before him requesting a glass of white wine,
he glared at me, baffled. I understood his bewilderment.
With a shrug and a look of disgust
he gave me the glass of wine.

Early morning of the fifth day, two of the young men,
solemnly, almost ceremoniously, picked me up
and, with dignified demeanor, dropped me off at the airport.

A Museum Hallway

I face a long hallway—well lighted and
with regal chairs against one wall
and paintings hung on both walls.
I move along, pausing to study each painting.
 A Toucan in a tree looking about for his next move.
A bridge of yellow stone, grown old with moss,
destroyed during World War Two.
The face of a pious monk looking skyward.
A formation of sparrows in flight
All, except one, headed in the same direction.
That one is confused, flying in circles.

After a Few Drinks

After a few drinks his hands get restless
as he reaches for parts of her above and under the table
and the bouncer isn't noticing anyway.
The crowded ballroom is noisy with laughter, music, and chatter,
and full of bright colors from strobe lights moving around and around,
so who cares except maybe the half-drunk woman herself
who has her own agenda she's long held back on such occasions
because first she wants to know if the guy is serious.
For years she's been on the lookout for a serious man
who can love her for herself, for her intelligence, not her body,
and this guy, reaching under the table,
is hardly a candidate for seriousness.
She's almost at the point where she's going to give in
and as usual place her search for mister serious on hold
and in the morning, she will hate herself for having done so.

FALL

It's reassuring to see the sturdy seagulls
perched on poles in a row along the pier.
They look so optimistic!
We're out for a stroll—to breathe the ocean air.
The horizon is high along the sky.
This time of year, when summer has gone
and winter is not yet here,
the tide is restless—like an animal
suddenly caught in a trap.
But we're careful where we walk.
When we reach the rocks, we stop,
grateful to be here, alive, and well,
and we sit down to rest.

THE CATHEDRAL

The cathedral down the river
a half mile away looms up high majestically
against the white skyline
like some rigid creature squatting there
since the Paleolithic Age.
I've walked from here along the river
among the tourists to it
and entered its hallowed space,
with sunlight coming in
through stained glass windows.
Inside, I always feel speechless—awe-struck.
Perhaps it's the majestic power of the place.

The Old Hut

The old hut, shed or shack—call it what you will.
Once clearly seen, it is barely visible now.
Vines and shrubbery and undergrowth
and young trees too,
like an ironic blessing from nature,
have all but covered it. Only a portion
of the path to the door,
and the door itself, are visible.
The sunrises and sets
still finding its way to that door
and to the growth surrounding it.
On the way here I walked
through the opening in the stone wall.
I'm not surprised that everything here has changed.
No longer charming in the earlier way.
It's now charming in a new way.

Like Dreamtime

As the holiday approaches I brace myself
for the disruption of pattern and its comfort and reassurance—
it's like preparing to throw myself into the melee,
the unpredictability of Dreamtime—with its dead
coming back to life and sashaying among the living,
building bonfires to scare off the ghosts,
or chopping down trees and bringing them into the house.
I grit my teeth and get through it,
grateful when it's in the rearview mirror,
way down the road receding around the curve,
but I know it's only a matter of time.

MANNERS

As a kid I chopped up my spaghetti,
but in Italy I learned to eat spaghetti
the way my Italian friend, Lorenzo, ate spaghetti.
You pick up a forkful, lift it above your head,
with your head thrown back, mouth wide open—like a baby bird,
you feed the strings together into your open mouth,
chewing it as it feeds in. It's an unsightly thing to do
in public in America—where people wrap spaghettini round a fork
and eat it that way—and at first, I was a bit embarrassed
to eat it Lorenzo's way in public, but now I don't care,
I do it in the finest American restaurants
with people looking at me in amazement,
no doubt thinking how boorish, how ill-bred, how uncouth,
but just today at lunchtime, at a fine restaurant at the next table
everybody was eating their spaghetti by lifting it high on a fork
and feeding it into their open mouths.
I think I've started something.

LUNCHEON

Friends are coming over.
At the dining room table, with its white tablecloth,
my wife is setting the table. Six plates. A platter of shellfish.
A huge bowl of tossed salad. A big basket of fresh bread.
Fresh spring water in pitchers. White and red roses
from the garden in the middle. Canisters of red and white wine
at each end. Bowls of fruit. A window is open
to let in the breeze from the garden.
They should start arriving soon,
bringing the pleasure of their company.

NIGHT LIGHTS

We're in a Chinese restaurant eating dinner and I look out.
I love the busyness of the night street.
A slender woman rushes along carrying a big black umbrella.
City darkness decorated with a lively sprinkle of lights.
Happy to see people out shopping, buying flowers from the corner vendor,
and now it is starting to rain slightly, and now harder and harder,
as umbrellas go up. Lights inside a long line of shopwindows
on the other side, one after another turning brighter.
People rushing for shelter of the elevated tracks
as a train rumbles by above—*clackety-clack.*
Across the street, on the corner in front of the drugstore
a newsboy is selling newspapers—"Get your *Daily News!*"
A woman holds onto her hat as she bumps through the crowd
going down the steep steps to the busy subway.
Out at sea a foghorn blasts a warning to an approaching ship.

THIS STRETCH

This stretch of northern California, flesh-colored
green-growing, brown starving, thirsty-dry.
The Pacific with its crashing waves,
responding and sky responding to both.
The stretch rugged and vibrantly alive with thick hills
pregnant valleys, dunes, snow, and fake snow,
lonely plains, exaggerated boulders, majestic mountains,
skies full of grayish smeared-on rainclouds
ready to nourish this stretch—a stretch of starving earth.
It endures fires and impatiently waits for rain.
I lay down patiently in its arms
and gaze up at a sky full of toothpaste clouds.

Printmaking

The printmaker carefully peels
a heavy sheet off the metal plate.
A family summer gathering—
husband and wife or
mother and father—girl and boy.
Girl on mother's lap.
Boy on father's lap.
They're on a grassy hillside.
A mountain looms in the distance.
The printmaker applies
a fresh sheet to the metal,
waits for an image to take,
lifts it slowly. The colors
are smoother, less intense,
more in harmony with the tones,
the feeling of family, deeper.
Numbered and signed.

Vacation Rental

The cat likes to sit on my lap and purr.
Acrobats on TV are still at it,
leaping and turning three times
in midair before landing on their feet.
They're skilled optimists.
The man next door is pushing an electric lawnmower
back and forth across dead grass.
I know there's budding life beneath that deadness,
where the roots are. I'm also an optimist.

VACATION

On vacation in Hawaii for the first time
we lay on the beach,
but that was not enough to feel like vacation,
so we went shopping, but that too was not enough

to feel like vacation.
We drove up a mountain toward a volcano,
but halfway up, the road got narrow—it felt dangerous,
so we turned back. We wondered what people do

on vacation to feel like vacation.
We weren't feeling it.
We went back to the beach
and lay on the sand till it was time to fly home.

There was nothing else to do,
nowhere else to go.

In Balboa Park

I saw her at the other end of the plaza.
I thought I knew her from years ago—in New York,
 a woman who had fled the city
out of fear she might be deported.
I'd wondered for years where she'd gone.
Had she returned to her native country
or stayed in America and run off to another state?
My gaze was unwavering
as I tried to see if she was my long-ago friend.
The woman noticed I was staring at her.
While holding a slight smile—
no doubt from feeling flattered by the attention—
she slowly started walking toward me.
When she was within about five feet,
I could see she was not my friend from years before.
Something also changed in her face—
perhaps because something had changed in mine.

FISHERMAN'S WHARF

Friday night in winter
we embarked at Oakland
sailing across the freezing Bay
and disembarking at Pier 45
and in a wharf restaurant
we ate delicious clam chowder hot
and steaming Dungeness crab.
Early next morning on TV
black smoke billowing up from
La Rocca Seafood warehouse
where fish is processed and stored,
walls collapsed, smoke quickly drifting out
across waterfront to old SS *Jeremiah* of Normandy
glory, docked there.
Firefighters on the way.

EYEGLASSES

Going through customs at Accra,
the officer opens my briefcase
and pulls out an eyeglass case.
He opens it and sees a pair of eyeglasses—
my reading glasses.
Puzzled, he looks up at my face
and the glasses I'm wearing.
Why does this man need two pairs of glasses?
He continues to search the briefcase
and comes up with another pair—
my distance glasses.
Again, he looks up, even more puzzled.
Is this man smuggling eyeglasses?
He shrugs and continues to search the briefcase
till he finds my sunglasses. Still confused,
he returns everything to the briefcase
and disgustedly pushes it to me
while turning to the next person in line.

THE LEFT-HANDED CAR

A week in Jamaica! In Kingston
I rented an Austin (the steering wheel
on the right side—British, the only kind available).
My first left-handed car! Being left-handed,

driving a left-handed car felt natural.
I drove up to the northern coast
where the Spanish once ruled.
The drive up the long winding road

through a profusion of trees
and undergrowth, through Nine Mile town,
while listening to Bob Marley singing,
was mysterious and exciting.

I arrived at Ocho Rios—a sunny day.
I bought ice cream and stood on the sidewalk eating it.
I was not interested in the beach,
nor the rainforest, nor the waterfall, nor the lagoon.

I was anxious to get back in my left-handed car
and get back on the road. Driving back, I was happy—
not stressed about anything. Back in Kingston
a young man offered to sell me marijuana.

I said no thanks. I was already high
on driving my left-handed car.
The more I drove it, the more I loved driving it.
I drove it to Montego Bay, on the north coast.

There, I was not interested in snorkeling,
nor the coral reef, nor the amusement park,
nor the beaches. I drove my left-handed car
to Port Antonio and there on the northwest coast

I gazed at the rippling blue water,
but didn't visit the tropical jungles nor the waterfalls.
I was anxious to get back in my left-handed car.
One day I drove it to Morant Bay—

took a quick look at the lighthouse, the falls,
the beach, then back to my left-handed car.
A whole week of driving left-handed. I loved it!
(Oh, yeah, I also loved Jamaica.)

WHISKY

The bartender is in the backroom
talking on her cellphone—
loudly and laughing.

The barroom is dark and damp
with a stream of daylight
coming through a side window.

I'm at the bar with a glass of beer.
Three elderly men, farmers,
across the room,

one standing, two seated,
at a table drinking beer and talking—
talking in low grumbling voices.

I can't hear what they're saying,
but mortality lurks behind the words.
At another table across the room,

a man and a woman—in their fifties:
he's reading a newspaper
and she's sitting there

with her elbows on the table
and her fists under her chin—
revisiting her early expectations.

I look up at the bottles of whisky
in perfect formation like cadets
neatly lined up on two long shelves

behind the bar—about a hundred.

BENCHES

Here in the park the benches are hard and sturdy.
Some are made of wood, others of stone. Some are dedicated by families
of loved ones now departed: *To the loving memory of . . .*
The old folks with longing in their eyes sit here every day.
They gaze at the children playing on the slides and monkey bars
and the ducks in the pond, the girl lying on her belly on the grass,
reading a book. They gaze at the astonishingly blue sky.
One bench says: *May you find peace here . . .*

Chopped Salad

Today, on my way to meet you for lunch,
I saw a long line of soldiers lined up
waiting to enter the hospital, some with amputated legs,
amputated arms, bandaged heads, some walking with crutches,
all looking unhappy, and I thought about war, its casualties,
and why it has been at the center of human activity
since the beginning of the species.
Men have been returning like these men
since before the days of Odysseus,
Achilles, Ajax, and Alexander the Great.
You ordered the Chopped Salad; I, the Greek.

Noon in the Park

On a strip of ice
along the sloping sidewalk
kids were running and sliding
and falling just as often,
falling and giggling—
a couple on a nearby bench
laughing at their antics.
Piles of snow along edges.
A flock of migrating birds unusually
high up flying south.
This was a hard winter in the city,
but to see these kids having fun
you would not know it.
You would not know it was noon either—
the distant sky a deep purple
with cumulus clouds
hanging over looming skyscrapers,
but here in the park
you could barely hear
the rumble of the commuter train
shooting along the elevated tracks
less than a mile away.

INDEPENDENCE

In the Bahamas I didn't do the limbo,
but I was tempted to.
I watched a skinny girl in a nightclub
bend backward and slow walk gracefully
under a long rod—as though she had no bones in her body.
My back would have snapped in two.
Prince Charles was arriving the next day
to formally announce the island independent from England.
The excitement was electric. Teenage boys climbed trees to see better.
That night Sidney Poitier ran across the stadium under the lights,
waving to the excited crowds in the stands.
Local officials made political speeches about the past and the future.
Morning came in over the ocean and we watched the
prince come down the gangplank from the ship, waving happily.
The formality was brief. Papers were signed and hands shaken.
The next day, after climbing the gangplank, he waved again.
We watched the ship slowly leave the harbor.
Confetti flew and music filled the streets.
To celebrate, John Canoe danced in the streets with us.
The Bahamas was now free!

Tradition

In our favorite Filipino restaurant,
the owner, happily and repeatedly, reminds us
that, when he retires—
(and he is gleefully looking forward to that day)—

he will quickly close the restaurant
and speedily return home to the Philippines—
where he wants to slowly live out his remaining days.
One day he asks me if,

when I retire from teaching,
will I return to the place where I was born?
I emphatically say no.
He looks puzzled.

Surely, he says, everyone returns home.
He has never heard of anyone not doing do.
I thought of a Muslim poet-friend in Yugoslavia
who, upon hearing that I was twice divorced,

was shocked and mystified.
He had never heard of such blasphemy.
That conversation was the unhappy beginning of the end
of the friendship we were forming.

In Africa once an African woman said to me
you Americans have no culture and no history.
She spat out those words in my face
with such venom I was stunned.

Unlike my Filipino friend, I felt liberated—and luckily so—
from the constraints of tradition.
Unlike my Muslim friend in Yugoslavia,
I felt liberated from the constraints of custom.

Unlike the African woman, I, as an American, had multiple
histories and multiple cultures—to sort and understand.
But how could I tell them this great news?
They would never have understood.

TRANSPORTED

My cousin talked me into coming.
The organ-grinder playing the organ slowly and expertly.
I'm eating cotton candy and watching.
Soon people will be dancing.
Tipsy and dressed in traditional garb,
the women, mothers and daughters and sisters,
from the kitchens and factories,
in long dresses are dancing cheek-to-cheek
with the drunk men—fathers and sons and brothers,
from the fields and factories too.
Sausage-and-onion breath kissing whisky-breath.
It is like being transported back to the 16th century.

TROUBLE IN THE DESERT

Williams said, "no one to drive the car,"
but I say no one to fix the car.
The hood is up
and we're looking at the engine,
the alternator, the belts, the oil cap,
the dipstick, the battery, the cylinders,
the radiator, the sparkplugs,
the pistons, the crankshaft,
the transmission, the reservoirs,
and we don't have a clue.
Put your beer down and come look.
The sun has dropped behind the hills
and soon it will be dark.
The batteries in the flashlight
in the glove compartment are dead.
We'll be in the dark out here
in the middle of nowhere.
Go back in the tavern
and get that woman
in the white evening gown.
She says she knows about cars.

TREE RINGS

Sitting alone on a decaying bench
in the hot sun, you, a lonely girl of
sixteen, daydreaming of happiness.
You would rather be at one of those luncheon tables

across the river with those beautiful people
facing the river with its bright sailboats drifting by,
but the trees providing shade
for those privileged people

are happier than the people will ever be.
Look at the trees waving their limbs and leaves
in the breeze coming in from the ocean.
Those trees can last hundreds of years.

This is happiness we can't achieve, but
we can imagine it. Imagination is heaven.

SUDDENLY

He was suddenly with us in Germany—
like a hummingbird to the top hollyhock.
Said he just happened to be there on business.

Then, on a sunny day,
he was suddenly with us in France.
Just there on business.

We went to Italy for almost a year.
He came to Italy many times
and saw us, he said, quite by chance—like the weather.

We went back to France.
He turned up again in France
and wanted to treat us to lunch.

We knew what was going on.
(Dinah Washington said
you must get up early in the morning

and go to bed late at night
before you can fool her.)
I think he knew we knew,

but it didn't matter.

The Necessity of Water

In that Spanish village where I stopped
to fill my water canister at a well
women were coming there with clay water jugs
balanced perfectly on the tops of their heads.
They wore long dresses and shawls thrown around their shoulders.
Their hair was pulled back in a tight bun
at the back of their necks.
They filled the jugs then a boy stationed there
helped them place the jugs back on their heads
and they walked home perfectly straight, spilling none.
The boy smiled at me and said it was perfect for posture.

The Prime Mover

Alfredo ran the puppet show we all loved.
We knew he was back there behind the curtain,
manipulating the movement of the dolls,
but we loved pretending they were moving on their own.
They had such quaint and charming life
in their little ancient suits and hats and gowns and necklaces,
life in a different time and place,
a faraway country where people spoke a language strange to our ears,
a place from another time we loved daydreaming about.
Alfredo spoke for them all,
changing his voice for each individual one,
lowering his voice to different levels,
for the male characters—bass, baritone, tenor,
and raising it to higher and higher levels
for the females—soprano, mezzo-soprano, contralto.
He even did a great castrato.
Alfredo was completely convincing.
He was funny! We laughed and laughed.
He was ironic and never stale or dull.
Only once we were brought to tears—
when Rita died of a broken heart.
Only once!

THE GOAT GIRL

It's a scorched and windless day in the mountains.
The Colorado colors are burned-out blue and rust.
Eternally, the goats live for now—not the past, not the future.
They know the girl in her washed-out cotton dress
that hangs on her like a flower sack.
They come to her readily, their little tails
standing straight up like their little nubby horns
jutting up from the top of their heads.
They make their little goat-sounds
of anticipation and curiosity.
Their intense bodies say one thing:
did you bring something good to eat?
Except this time, she has not come with food.
She has come to play. She's nostalgic
for when they were does and kids.

REBELLION

From up here on the fifteenth floor
I see the city stretched out below.
People down there at a farmer's market
buying apples, figs, squash, green beans,
freshly baked bread, you name it,
a long line of parked cars they came in,
and across the tracks, the next street
where a man is entering a bank
to make a deposit or withdrawal.
Above and beyond him, in the distance,
the steeple of a church set against a bright blue sky.
I look down sharply at the building next door
and see through a window a woman inside sitting
at a desk typing at a computer. She's writing a novel.
It's inspired by her life, but it's not autobiographical,
it's fiction—the kind that rises to a higher truth:
girl growing up in small town, loss of innocence, coming of age,
rebellion against expectations.
Cinch to be a bestseller!

Shopwindows

Lighted shopwindows at night.
You and your friends leave the restaurant,
after a delicious and happy meal,
and you walk along the avenue
till you come to a brightly lighted window
full of color. You stop and gaze
at the fancy mannequins in their bright garments.
Farther along you come to another window
full of sparkling jewelry and tribal figurines.
You gather there and marvel.
You continue till you decide to stop for ice cream or coffee,
and you enter a café, and you fill the booth
and the waitress comes with a smile
and takes your orders
and as you wait for ice cream or coffee,
you wonder how on earth can you sustain
this fleeting moment of joy.

ROADSIDE RESTAURANT: ALL YOU CAN EAT

A lot here is just for show, and service is slow.
It's too much like photorealism—too real to be.
Hamburgers and fries look better than they taste.
The music is from the fifties—
Fats Domino, Little Richard, Elvis, Patsy Cline.
The Men's Room is dirty.
A big family, nevertheless, has come to dine.
You know the scene—Yachty Yak and Tutti Frutti.
I could listen all day—as if I had nothing better to do.

RENTING

Coming in, the first thing I noticed
just inside the front door, was the stairlift and the piano
near the foot of the stairs. I played the piano a bit.
I didn't try the stairlift. I knew it was for the wife.
Someone said she was an invalid.
The husband taught at the university.
They were away in Europe for the academic year.
We never met them.
We were renting the house for the semester.
The upstairs was dark and sparse.
Downstairs—the living room and the dining room
and even the kitchen—was lively and light.
We slept in the brighter of the three upstairs bedrooms.
Once we had houseguests. They took the middle bedroom,
the darkest and most depressing.
When they made love, it sounded like animals fighting—
one big animal trying to kill a smaller,
whimpering animal. I felt sorry for her.
During the day I looked at her sad face.
When she tried to smile, she could barely manage it.
Leaving, we left a *thank you* letter on the kitchen table.

The Pianist

The pianist wearing a blazer and yellow earrings
to match her yellow blouse
is at the piano, playing with such ease
she doesn't have to look at the keys,
instead, she looks back over her shoulder at us
in the room to see in our eyes who among us
is enjoying her music and we all are.
Her confidence is so obvious
as the keys ripple and the music fills the room.
The sheet music is propped on the piano for her to see,
but she doesn't need it.
It's simply there because that is where it belongs.

The Circus Is in Town

Today at an outdoor table at Starbucks
I sat with my cappuccino two tables away from a clown.
He was sitting alone with a serious face, serious—not sad.
His face was painted white and his lips a bright red.
He wore a big floppy hat matching the white of his clothes.
His clown suit was checkerboard red and white.
He was thoughtful and pensive—mentally somewhere else,
his latte on the table in front of him, no longer steaming.
I admired his courage and wanted to tell him so.
But respectful of his privacy I didn't dare disturb him.

ANOTHER REALM

This is that moment in the glow of bright lights,
as we stand under the marquee,
where the names of the movie and the names of the stars,
in blazing blinking lights, are flashing.
We stop, dazed and happy, as if we're about to enter
some elevated time and space, a place of magic,
and maybe we're about to do just that.
Before entering the foyer, we gaze at stills behind glass.
Inside, with a box of popcorn in hand,
we settle down in the cool darkness
halfway back from the big screen,
ready to be transported or transformed.
The movie starts and we're lifted out of ourselves
into another realm by the bigness of moving images,
and sound larger than life, in which we live for two hours.

A Dead Child

I had a dream about the Day of the Dead.
It was not like the festival in Mexico
or like the Catholic All Saints' Day
or All Souls Day on November first and second,
with families and friends gathering
to remember dead relatives and friends,
praying as the wall between the dead and the living
falls away, sharing the same world,
offering the dead tamales and chicken enchiladas,
pumpkin pie, cookies, and chocolate.
They visit cemeteries
and decorate the graves of loved ones,
but in my dream, everybody wore animal costumes
with pigfaces and cow-faces and horsefaces
and they dressed in sixteenth century costumes.
They marched through the village,
beating drums and tambourines,
carrying a small coffin containing a dead child,
all the while chanting and singing
songs I did not understand.

Reading

The room is dark the walls are dark,
the ceiling and floor are in shadows.
The only light—from a lamp high
on the dresser—shines down
on pages. I no longer exist.
I've entered the story.

PUZZLE

Through the kitchen window I see the lake frozen.
Overcast so thick impossible to see where the sky begins.
Things so frigid, hard to believe winter's giving birth to spring.
You sit at the square table by the window
with a yellow pencil in hand, poised over a crossword puzzle.
You're wearing an ancient pullover
of indeterminate color. Nowadays
you're also sporting your hair cut short.
Your coffee cup half full and no longer hot—
a lipstick smear on the rim—like a red streak across the sky.

H₂O

In Saint Paul de Vence we stop
where women and children are gathered
round a fountain gazing at bubbling water
as it recirculates. We too become mesmerized
by the moving water. Somewhere on one of the islands,
despite the danger of the sea overcoming the land,
a family is buying a home near the sea
so they can gaze at the moving waves.
A young man in California is riding big waves.
He goes up and down with them. He's having a great time.
A well-dressed woman in New York
stands in the shelter of an entryway waiting for the rain to stop.
A young man comes along, tips his hat to her, and offers her his umbrella.
She says no, thank you—but with a smile.

CHECKERS

They had their paper cups of steaming hot coffee
sitting on the sidewalk beside them.
The two engaged in the game were focused intensely
on the moves they needed to make.
The four or five others stood watching.
The onlookers could not advise either of the two players
on strategy or otherwise. That was the unspoken rule.

Automation

An old woman across from me sits with arms folded across her lap,
her purse tightly held beneath her hands, one on top of the other.
She's just had her hair cut and styled. She wishes she was home taking a nap.
Across from her another woman with a babyface under a funny bonnet,
gazes contentedly across the aisle at me. The young woman in lace
behind her has just married and is possibly pregnant.
The years go by. There is a glow on her face, slightly cocked to the side
like a dog looks when it's trying to understand you.
Outside the window the tunnel rushes by and the clanging rings in my ears.
The man with a cap pulled down over his eyes wants no part of this journey.
It's like we're in flight waiting to land. We're all patiently waiting for our stop,
a chance to see if our legs will still work when we stand.

Is the World an Apple?

Cezanne said the world is an apple—
or did I only imagine he said it?
In that world his descendants stumbled upon Cubism
and through its lens
happily, gave us beautifully twisted
and gloriously distorted noses, mouths, eyes, bellies—
especially pregnant bellies,
big feet, big hands, stylized skulls,
medicine bowls,
boobs the size of watermelons.
Look at these—
a missionary in Africa holding a bible
while ministering to a pregnant woman
with a baby on her back,
a mulatto wearing a halo
of hair and a necklace to match,
Kirchner's Milly sleeping on a red bed,
naked dancers singing,
Nelly showing a white woman
how to do that African step,
Sam getting ready to pose for Ernst,
but the winner is Vallotton's black woman
in blue culottes—a parody of Manet's *Olympia*.
She has a little red cap
and a cheap red necklace around her neck.
You can't beat that unlighted cigarette

dangling from her mouth.
She's sitting at the foot of the bed
gazing matter-of-factly
up at the sleeping naked woman with red hair.
You can just hear what she's thinking.

THE COMFORT OF BOOKS

Just knowing that they are there,
seeing them there,
even the ones not yet read, give comfort.
From ceiling to floor on library-type shelves,
those adjustable kind, light green in color, the shelves give order.
The books stand back-to-back,
tall ones together and so are the shorter ones,
sometimes arranged by type,
novels together, poetry together,
but not in alphabetic order.
I've never had the patience to do alphabetical.
Friends come and the first thing they ask is:
Are they in alphabetical order?
It's like, is your puppy house-trained.
No, they are not alphabetical,
but they are in order enough.
I know roughly where everything is
and have little trouble finding anything I wish to find.
The books give a comfort
like that of insurance, life insurance,
or like the alarm system you have on
while you are sleeping,
or like the security latch you secure
inside your hotel room,
especially before you go to sleep.

A QUICK BEER

When I turned twenty-one,
I went to a bar and sat there and ordered "scotch on the rocks,"
a drink I knew about from reading novels.
I found the first sip repulsive,
but I was determined to drink it
because that was what adults did.
Taverns and bars have long been a gathering place
where people socialize, drink, eat, fight, flirt, gossip,
hook up and use the toilet repeatedly.
Many years later, in Mexico, at dusk,
I walked into a tavern with a cement floor, and ordered a beer,
and was transported back to the eighteenth century.
The bartender was behind the bar pouring rum into a canister.
Barrels of rum and beer lined the walls, bottles of whisky were in rows
on shelves reaching to the ceiling.
A gaslamp hung from that ceiling. Three tradesmen were at a table
discussing what they should charge for the barrels they'd just delivered.
A lone man at another table finished his whisky and fell asleep
with his face on his folded arms, a sombrero pulled down over his eyes.
Men were beginning to come in from the fields, dusty and thirsty for rum.
It was a unique, and disquieting, moment—like my first drink.

Sleep

Here in a side room off the main room of the library
I sit by a tall window with a rounded top,
admiring the builder who took the trouble
to create this interesting architectural feature.
I scan the books on the shelves.
They stand back-to-back
like ancient dead soldiers in their tombs
waiting silently to be excavated
or to be read by a lonely boy
from the sixteenth floor of a high-rise in the Bronx.
The woman across the table from me
has her head down on the book she was reading.
She is now asleep.
I imagine at home at night in the dark
in bed she is unable to sleep,
so she comes here every day,
knowing that if she starts reading a book, any book,
a travel book or a cookbook
or a book on wild plants of the Amazon,
she will easily fall asleep
and get the sleep she can never get
at home in bed in the dark.

Our Secret Market

It was a little market in a small remote campo.
We shopped there.
The tomatoes were bright red.
Lettuce fresh and crisp.
Only fish caught that morning.
No need to go to Market Garibaldi.
There, we were taken to be tourists.
In our little market they knew better.
Unemployed young men
hung out in doorways.
Restless teenage girls
strolled about arm-in-arm.
Children played on the cobblestones.
Old women bartered with sellers.
Bedsheets hung on lines stretching from
one upper window to another across the way.
The gray-haired bookseller
with an unlighted pipe in his mouth,
manned his little stand nearby.
Boatmen in the canal called out greetings.
The antique print seller came only
on Wednesdays. He did good business.
Just beyond the bookseller the jewelry seller.
No tourist was likely to venture there.

BICYCLES

The laundry women of this ancient village ride bicycles
and carry small bundles in the front basket
and the big ones on the back fender.
But at any moment the world can regress.
We can all tumble down the slope of history
like a Colorado rockslide blocking the road,
and like a line of cars waiting there,
we might have no idea how to back up
or how to go around the blockage
without falling into the valley.

GOING BACK

I didn't sleep well last night.
The repetitive sound of train wheels
on rails kept me awake.
Across from me, you are beautiful
wearing your colorful cap—
your basket of apples on the seat beside you.
I know you slept well because I watched you.
Now, out the window I see two women
in long dresses and straw hats gathering plums
fallen from trees of the forest. Beyond the trees,
a shack with a worn-out straw broom
leaning against a weathered wall.
A narrow stream running by—
yellow from scum and sunlight.
I close my weary eyes and let the metallic sound
of wheels on rails—the same sound
that kept me wake—lull me to sleep.

Shoes

It's 10 a.m. and the shoe repair shop just opened.
The cobbler is hanging the *Open* sign in the window.
A little bell over the door rings when you enter.
You can now see him and his wife
through the window working on shoes.
He fits the shoe over the iron support
and hammers the tap onto the heel.
Inside, it smells of leather and dust.
On the shelves you see shoe cleaners,
socks, shoelaces, shoehorns, shoe polish
and shoe brushes, for sale.
His father and his grandfather ran this shop.
Back in those days
they repaired badly worn shoes and boots,
sewing, and gluing them
when and where necessary.
Nowadays the cobbler, not yet sixty,
will dye shoes or boots for you,
but he does mostly heel and toe taps.
If a pair of shoes are old enough to repair,
he is likely to tell you, you need to buy new shoes.
That was the message he gave me
when I took in my favorite pair of red suede shoes,
relics from my Rock 'n' Roll days.
If you walk by the shop at night
you will see a light glowing in there
as if from an altar.

WINNING

When it was slightly dark
and we were playing Hide and Seek,
I happened to look up
at a lighted window
where men in porkpie hats shading their eyes
were gathered around a table.
One was my Uncle George.
The window was open.
They were mostly silent.
Occasionally one would say *tilt*
or *rainbow* or *rags* or *all-in*
or *backdoor* or *call* or *check*
or draw or *flop* or *fold*
or *gutshot-straight* or *kicker.*
I understood none of the terms,
but I knew they were playing a game,
maybe playing it with cards,
not in a way we kids played cards.
When we played cards
it was for fun,
and we didn't hide our eyes
and we talked and laughed constantly,
and, as I suppose it was with them,
for us, it was important to win.

Lake Tahoe

Now summer, a high wind smelling of pinewood sap.
The same air you inhaled while roughing it elsewhere.
Barefoot we run across white sand warmed by midday sun
to water's edge. Out into clear water splashing we rush.
It's a stretch of clear blue as far as the eyes can see—
alpine clear. Water clear as glass rushes downstream
over ancient rocks smooth and rounded
in clusters, going only where water can go.

CROSSING THE PARK

On my way home at dusk, I cut through the park.
It's winter and it's raining with a strong wind whipping trees
and my umbrella sideways as I hurry along a footpath
through the park, passing empty benches,
where on a sunny day elderly friends and strangers
sit and talk about the future and the past,
and which shop makes the best bagels.
Ahead of me, an elderly man walking his dog.
Everyone needs to get home.
In the distance along the avenue tall buildings
blend as a solid shadow in the haze of the rain,
with an occasional light in an occasional window
along the line. Thankfully, one light is mine.

Sojourner Truth's Tiny Eyeglasses

Sojourner Truth, in her white skullcap,
with her white shawl thrown across her shoulders,
looks out at us through her granny glasses.
I'm sure she can see us, see us clearly.
I look at her through my new glasses,
I see her delicate hands moving with the ball of thread
and knitting needles. Through my distance glasses
her elbow touches the tiny Bible to her left.
Through my reading glasses she almost smiles.
Through my sunglasses she speaks,
"I sell the shadow to support the substance."
Yes, she sees us clearly and dearly—
and the vote, not just for men,
but for women too, is on her mind—
and rightly so.

Releasing

Outside next door, with much banging,
workers are putting up a new fence
between our yard and our neighbor's yard.
Frost said good fences make good neighbors.
They were good neighbors before the new fence.
The old fence, as shabby as it was, served its purpose.
In one's life, little improvements are interesting,
though not always seen as such.
Just before moving one wonders
if moving is going to end with good result.
Dancing seems to improve with music.
Writing poetry improves when you stop thinking:
what kind of poems should I write?
The poem is already there. It just needs to be released—
so that it finds its natural place.

Chalk Marks on the Sidewalk

A rubber ball lays on the bottom step beside
a toy truck with one wheel missing.
A rope with plastic handles hangs on the banister.
The children have stopped laughing,
jumping rope and playing hopscotch.
They sit solemnly on the front steps in hazy afternoon sunlight.
One looks down at ants crawling along a crevice,
another holds his face in his hands, gazing at nothing.
The word *funeral* is still ringing in their ears.
Two boys stand by the railing,
leaning on it as if they need something
to keep them from falling over.

The Spanish Civil War

In 1954 I was in the Air Force,
being trained for clerical work.
I lived in a barracks with men from the Spanish Air Force
in training also at clerical school,
on a base outside Cheyenne. In typing class,
they horsed around. The instructor was amused
by their antics. Some were from the north,
others, the south. They were, playfully, still fighting
the Spanish Civil War, 1936–1939.
The bone of contention—the failed coup
to overthrow King Alfonso, the Thirteenth.
Long story shorter—Spain got stuck with fascist Franco.
He was still in power when in '71 I first visited Spain.
In Barcelona I remembered my Spanish roommates.
They wrestled on the beds, sometimes tumbling to the floor,
playfully, happy warriors.

GRIEF

We know the horrors of lynching
and nailing people to the cross
throughout human history, but not much
about the grief felt by you when you
come to dismount the body. Grief grabs your face
and turns you into a mask of suffering.
Your trembling hands wrap the body in a blanket
you remembered to bring. You struggle,
carrying it to safety, and a final resting place.
The dead lives in you for as long as you live.

FEAR AND LONGING

When I lived in the city,
at dusk, I sometimes went up to the roof
to watch the sunset. The city haze and smoke
mixed with the bright red sun going down
made long ripples across the sky.
It was always dramatic with the tall dark buildings,
now only blunt shadows standing in sharp contrast
against the early night. A woman from the third floor
was often there hanging up clothes on clotheslines—
bedspreads, pillowcases, baby diapers. With tears in her eyes,
she would stop and gaze longingly at the sky.

CROSSING THE STREET

Here she comes now,
dressed for summer, but it's winter,
unsure of her own name and her next step,
as she begins unsteadily to cross the street.
Catch her—*hurry*!
You take one hand and I'll take the other.

THE VIRUS

I had to balance my brother on my shoulders
to make him tall enough to read the rules (otherwise
known as laws to live by) held high
by the holier-than-thou rulers (otherwise
known as demigods or demons in the guise of gods).
The punishment for not reading them
and living by them
was unknown, but you didn't want to have to find out.
If you got *that* involved,
you were already doomed. Best to stay innocent (otherwise
known as dumb). Evidence was clear all about:
skulls. Stacks of skulls. Piles of bones.
Once I held him up, it was his turn
to hoist me upon his shoulders.
Such was our uncertain life during the plague (otherwise
known as the virus) then and now.

THE RICH GIRL AND HER CHAUFFEUR AT THE CAFÉ

In pastel colors and smelling of the best cologne,
twelve, she's fancy dressed in her Sunday-best
and sits leaning back with her little legs crossed.
She's finishing her ice cream soda and is beginning to look restless.
In his new uniform, and driving cap, Francisco,
her chauffeur, sits next to her patiently, watching and
waiting for her next move. He knows she's impulsive.
Where will she want to go next? The circus or the zoo?
He knows her better than she will ever know him.

A Place on the Way

Years ago, on the way down
during a car trip from Venice
to Vetri, we stopped overnight
at a little "residence"

run by an elderly couple.
I made a sketch of the olive trees
alongside the wall
between the vineyard and the patio.

The residence was very charming, very quaint.
We had a nice little room with a stone floor.
We ate our meals outside on the patio.
But now it is a big fancy resort

with horseback riding and swimming—
you name it, they've got it.
Dining is inside with fancy napkins.
Alas, it's no longer cheap and charming.

I'm told the beds are now firm
and the owners are new people—
Glad we knew the place
before it became successful.

Things You Can Do

You can ride a runaway bull and not fall.
You can comfort a weeping old woman.
You can wrestle a rival in the arena and win.
You can look longingly through your jail bars.
You can calm an angry crowd with the right words.
If you want, you can be the bull, not the bullfighter.
You can help take the body down from the cross.
You can sprout gigantic flapping wings
and fly around in the night air till sunrise.
You can carry your crazy brother on your back.
With your accordion you can be the Hurdy Gurdy Man.
You can remove the dunce hat from
the legless man and give him crutches.
You can carry the donkey on your back or ride the donkey.
You can be Daedalus catching Icarus as he falls.
You can play Blind Man's Bluff dancing in a circle
or you can be the blind "man" in the circle.
You can ride a bucking horse and not fall.
You can show the others the way out of the camp before
the bandits, with their toy guns, come on their exhausted horses.
With pie you can comfort a fasting monk in his dungeon.
You can walk on extra-long stilts or throw them away.

Night in the City

Children, counting and calling,
running on the sidewalk—high-rise kids
playing hide-and-seek under streetlights.
Apartment window-lights flicking on.
The belltower clock says seven.
It's beginning to rain,
storefront lights across the street
reflecting in wet asphalt.
A woman at the bus stop opens an umbrella.
A firetruck goes by screaming.
Somebody shouts from a window
there's a fire in the factory down the street.
The beggar woman walks by
with arms folded across her chest.
Avoiding her, a man wearing a top hat
opens a taxi door for two young women
in heels and feather hats
as they ease into the backseat.
Up on the roof, in a gray housecoat,
with clothespins in her mouth,
a woman snatches laundry from a clothesline.

First Light

The donkeys and mules are packed,
and the treasure-hunters are ready
to trudge into the hills and mountains
to search the creeks and hillsides for gold.
You think this ended in the 19th century?
Think again. They're still doing it.
I've seen it first-hand in the hills of Colorado.
The animals are loaded with provisions
and the men have heavy backpacks
strapped to their backs. A wife waves goodbye
from an upper window. Another is hanging morning wash.
Will they come back with gold?
In the casino the House is the biggest winner.
In the hills, nature is the House.

A Memory

They stop and stand—all of them—
as if a photographer is aiming a camera at them.
The old man, with his wide-brimmed hat pulled down low
to shade his eyes, looks as if he's about to take another step away.
The two old women, in their long heavy dresses and aprons,
stand slightly in the background.
The teenage boy, in front,
looks at the jackrabbit hopping across the road
disappearing into the underbrush.
The mountain range behind them is gray,
same color of the sky, and the earth they're standing on.

STUDIO

They're dressed in suits and neckwear.
With a probing look, the bearded art teacher
stands arrogantly in front.

The only person conspicuously naked is the model.
She stands proudly alongside the teacher—not smiling.
She's holding a palette that serves as a fig leaf.

Yes, even in 19th century Paris
a fig leaf was sometimes necessary,
though the classic nude was long dead.

Manet's woman with eyes wide open,
rather than demurely lowered,
looking at us, ended the classic reign.

And the teacher—you know who—
was always ready to put himself forward.
That is why, if, in a hotel lobby,

he was waiting for you to arrive,
and you've never met before,
as you came in from the street,

you would spot him right away—
the one standing, impatiently
looking at his wristwatch.

THE *Americain*

In Haiti the hotel manager assigned me a taxi driver, Henri,
to shepherd me around Haiti—
without a shepherd, he said, *you might run into trouble.*
One day Henri drove me up into the hills to a market.
I got out and walked through the market. Little polite boys,
dignified as well-brought-up royalty, followed me
along the rows of yams, cabbage, onions, beets, tomatoes,
carrots, and plantains, begging to be my guide.
I kept handing them money and saying no thanks,
but the boys kept coming. They followed me back to the taxi.
Henri called out to them, "*Pas plus—va-t'en!*"
And, looking sad and crestfallen, they scattered.
But I loved those boys! I was sad to see them back off,
waving goodbye to me—their *Americain*.

At Sea

We've stopped at a little burger joint alongside the road
and my wife, tired, behind big sunglasses
and with a bright scarf round her hair,
while picking something out of her teeth,
says, "I hate traveling, hate it, hate it!"
We're sitting at an outdoor table,
a table with names and dates and heart-shapes
carved into its top. I remind her this trip was her idea.
Yeah, she says, it was, it was, but there is such a suspended feeling,
a feeling I didn't expect, a feeling of being unmoored,
adrift at sea with no home, no safety.
"When did travelling become like this?"

Scarecrow

My neighbor built a makeshift scarecrow
and stuck it on top of the shack
out back of his house.
Its arms flapped around loosely,
in the wind from the hills,

like he was waving away crows,
but the crows were never fooled.
They perched on the scarecrow's head
 and sang *caw, caw, caw.*
It was a kind of victory song

that said take that you sucker
and to rub it in even more,
they pooped on the head.
My neighbor said
sometimes you just can't win.

After This Poem

A soldier is nursed back to health.
Swimmers are pulling themselves to shore to rest.
After running runners stop to catch their breath.
Removing a mask does not necessarily reveal a face.
When the speaker finishes speaking there will be questions.
After separation, reunion—maybe.
Can no one assure us contentment after longing?
After injury strive for recovery.
A storm recedes and the sun comes out.
Sex then conversation. No cigarette.
After loss there might be gain.
Silence can follow rage. It has happened.
Carnival now—dreamtime again next year.
After jeopardy—bereavement.
Swim to the bottom of the sea—see what's there.
This is the end of the line.

Hot Afternoon

I look up at the sky. It's full of movement.
It pushes down heating plowed land.
A little man, helpless, caught between the two,
struggles with a plow and a worn-out mule.
I sit here at Café's single outdoor table.
I'm watching him with compassion.
I'm watching the coastline and the sea—
where a boat, puffing smoke, is sailing upstream,
followed by a barge full of shrimp.

CLOTHESPINS

Sister Margaret, with clothespins (like carved wooden birds
with their wings folded firmly to their sides) in a basket
on the ground, reaches down for two pins at a time,
keeping one in her hand and placing the other in her mouth,
secures the sheet to the line with the wooden pin in her hand,
releasing the other one from her mouth to secure the other end,
repeating the process in an assembly-line fashion.
The other nuns, jokingly, call her "Mother Bird."

Outdoor Café Scene

He's wearing an ochre suit and a black bowtie.
He looks like an insect—with wings.
She's in a long red dress, blue heels.
A large floppy hat shading her eyes.
She's a large bird about to take off.
Self-consciously, she's looking south—
as if waiting for the arrival of someone.
He looks north, to avoid impolitely looking at her.
Their dogs, one sitting, the other, standing,
looking at each other with silent interest.

Her Parallel

She comes in from the cold morning
in overcoat and wool dress and sensible shoes.
They greet each other politely.
She hangs her coat on his coat rack by the door.
She goes behind the partition.
He is now standing at his easel
waiting for her to undress in privacy.
I find it interesting that the undressing itself is so private,
especially since she will emerge nude
in all her classic glory, but it is not this nakedness itself
that is worthy of privacy, only the undressing,
the preparation for the creation of her parallel,
a two-dimensional image that will hang in a public gallery
for all interested to see and admire.

STATIC

It's a door, white-washed
like the walls surrounding it.
Late sunlight pours in,
spilling in an oblong whiter shape
across the white stone floor.
The moment is filled with optimism,
expectation, possibility.
It's as though something—anything—
is about to happen.

The Famous Model

She knows she has the upper hand.
She's dressed too sharply for the occasion—
a grand silk-lined hat, a red cape,
and a long satin dress with blue and white trim.
She sits sedately in her chair
like an Egyptian figurine upright in a tomb.
leaning forward with one arm resting on the glass of the tabletop.
A bottle of Merlot near her elbow,
a bit of wine left at the bottom of her glass.
It glows like stardust.
She speaks singingly in a whisper—a siren voice.
To better hear her in earnest, in unison,
her men lean toward her—like well-trained soldiers.
She is smiling with each word—
it's as though she can taste the musical sounds
of the words coming out her mouth.
They each have a different color, too.
She knows she has the upper hand.
They know it too.

How the Republic Was Born

Five women in long black dresses sitting by a wall
shelling peas into aluminum pans know how the republic was born.
The old man mending shoes in the shoe shop next door
knows about Lucretia and how the republic was born.
The old woman at the window two doors down,
looking up at the Roman sky, with death in her eyes,
knows all about Lucretia and how the republic was born.
The woman in a cloak standing in a hallway two stories up,
unsure of which way to go, can tell you about Lucretia,
and how the republic was born.
Down the block the man cleaning fish at the fish market
knows how the republic was born.
Two women, across the alley, in the double swing, swinging,
can sing a song about Lucretia.
The scholar in the *scuola* by the bridge
knows how in 509 the republic was born. He's teaching his students
how the republic was born, hoping they will spread the news—
of how the republic was born.

GIBBET

Never forget Wilma of the 17th century,
in shabby clothes, with hands tied at her back
and an iron collar clamped around her neck—
like those used on slaves—
and attached to the gibbet to hold her head up.
She's chained by the neck to the gibbet.
Her legs bound with iron.
If someone tries in the night to free her,
they will have a difficult time
cutting through that metal.

IMPORTANT WORK

In spring and summer,
my two cousins and I made toy boats.
We constructed them out anything at hand—
cardboard or paper, a piece of soft wood,
the kind that floats, and after a heavy rain,
we sailed them in puddles.
In winter and fall we made toy trucks
out of anything we could find—pieces of scrap wood
or roofing fallen from a house,
and we hauled sand or blades of grass
that looked to us like the real thing—grain or hay,
that real truckdrivers haul. We had no doubt
we were doing important work.

Among Clarence Major's previous sixteen poetry collections are *Swallow the Lake* (a National Council on the Arts winner), *Configurations: New and Selected Poems* (a National Book Award Bronze Medal winner), and *Sporadic Troubleshooting* (2022). He has contributed poetry to the *New Yorker, Harvard Review, American Scholar, American Poetry Review, Best American Poetry, Literary Review, Ploughshares,* and dozens of other periodicals. A Fulbright scholar, among Major's other awards are a Western States Book Award, a Lifetime Achievement Award for Excellence in the Fine Arts from the Congressional Black Caucus Foundation, and a PEN Oakland/Reginald Lockett Lifetime Achievement Award for Excellence in Literature. He was elected to the Georgia Writers Hall of Fame in 2021. Major is a distinguished professor emeritus of twentieth-century American literature at the University of California, Davis.